My Little Golden Book About Route 66

By Diane Muldrow • Illustrated by Alexandra Bye

For the merchants, preservationists, and road-trippers who keep Route 66 humming
—D.M.

A GOLDEN BOOK • NEW YORK

Golden Books
An imprint of Random House Children's Books
A division of Penguin Random House LLC
1745 Broadway, New York, NY 10019
penguinrandomhouse.com
rhcbooks.com

Library of Congress Control Number: 2025933363
ISBN 978-0-593-90593-7 (trade) — ISBN 978-0-593-90594-4 (ebook)
Manufactured in the United States of America
10 9 8 7 6 5 4 3 2
EU Contact: Penguin Random House Ireland, 32 Nassau Street, Dublin D02 YH68.
https://eu-contact.penguin.ie

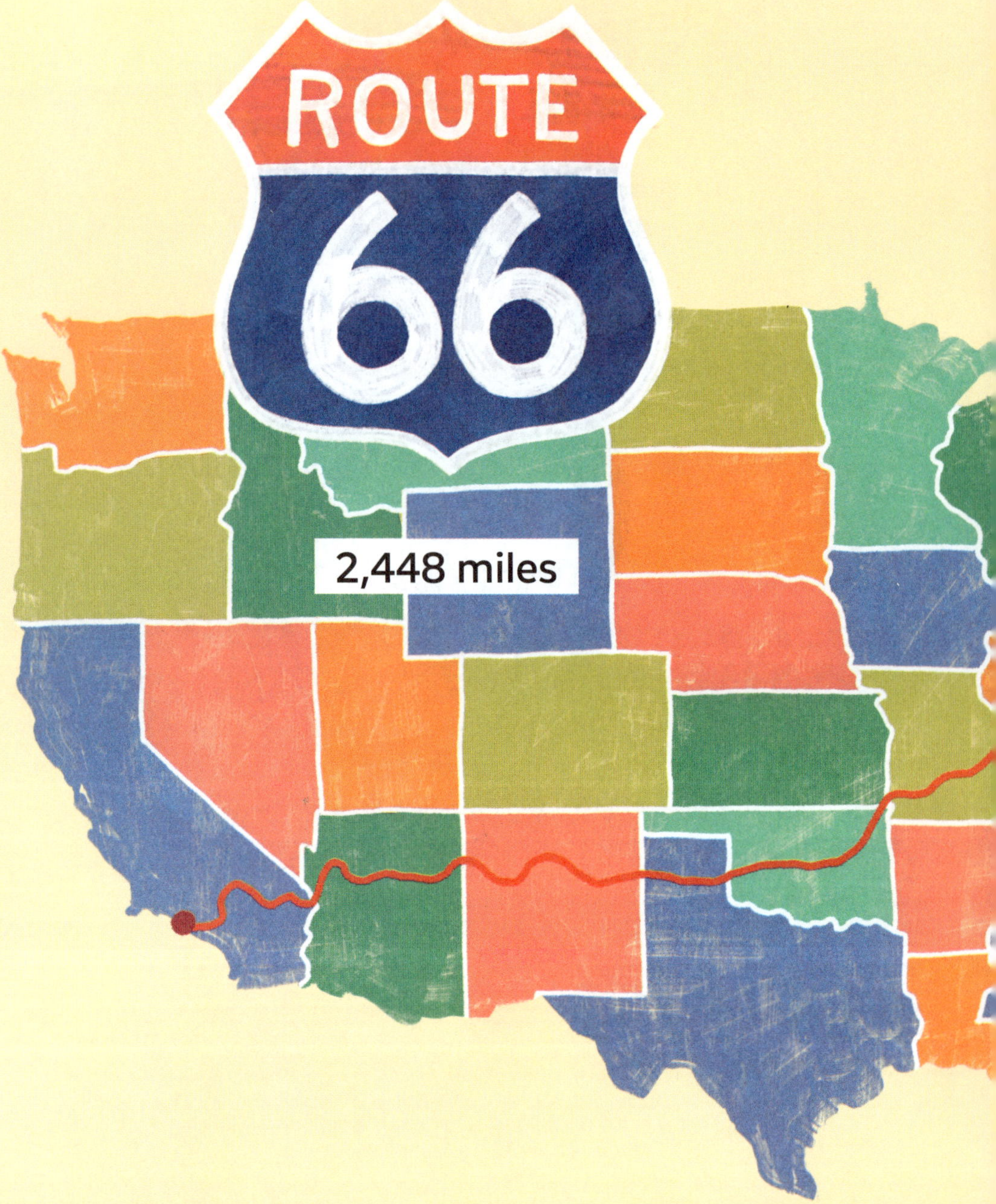
ROUTE
66
2,448 miles

Hi! I'm Ramblin' Rosie, and I'm revvin' up my engine to explore US Route 66. *Vroooooom!*

Route 66 is a hundred years old! It was the first paved road to connect people and goods from the Midwest all the way to the West Coast, over two thousand miles away. Sometimes people call it America's Main Street or the Mother Road. It's so famous that there's even a song about it that goes, *"Get your kicks on Route 66."*

The route begins in Chicago, Illinois. This big city has lots of skyscrapers. My favorite is the Willis Tower, behind me. You can visit its Skydeck—the highest observation deck in the US. On a clear day, you can see up to four different states!

Route 66 can lead you from one of the world's tallest buildings to . . .

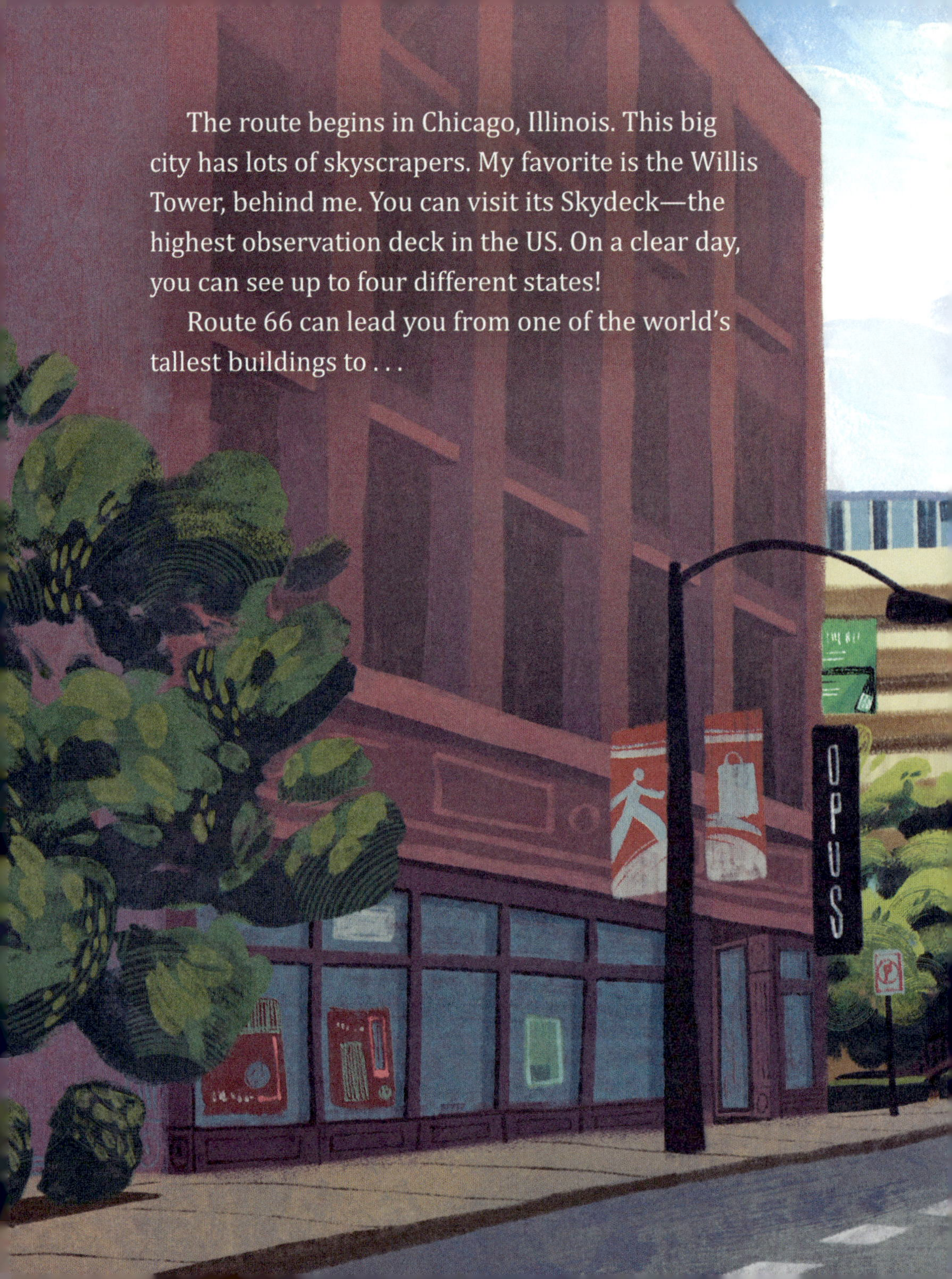

BEGIN
HISTORIC
ILLINOIS
U.S.
66
ROUTE

. . . the world's largest catsup bottle!

This water tower, in Collinsville, Illinois, is 170 feet tall. It was put up in 1949 to advertise a nearby catsup bottling plant, and people have loved it ever since.

Did the catsup bottle make you hungry? Good thing there are lots of cool places to eat along the Mother Road.

You can find a 1950s-themed diner where you can sip a milkshake in a comfy booth and listen to music from your own little jukebox!

Now, some folks would rather drive on those stick-straight interstates to get where they're going. Sure, they're faster, but I never did like being in a hurry. And I don't hit the road to see the same stores and fast-food joints that I can find any ol' place. Route 66 was designed to move around the natural curves of the beautiful American landscape. So let's head back out to see what's 'round the bend!

Speaking of curves, the Gateway Arch here in St. Louis, Missouri, surely is dramatic! It's the world's tallest arch. It stands in Gateway Arch National Park, the smallest national park in the US. You can take the four-minute tram ride to the top of the arch for a spectacular view—630 feet up!

Did you know that Missouri is called the Cave State? Here in Meramec Caverns in Stanton, Missouri, you can see the world's rarest and largest cave formations. They're the oldest attraction on Route 66—up to 400 *million* years old!

After Route 66 was created to be the shortest, safest, and most scenic route from Illinois to California, smart-thinking folks opened businesses to take care of the travelers. Some service stations were built to look like homey cottages—such as this adorable one in Baxter Springs, Kansas. It's now the Kansas Route 66 Visitors' Center.

Hit the brakes! Here's the famous Blue Whale of Catoosa, Oklahoma. Back in the 1970s, Mr. Hugh S. Davis built it for his whale-lovin' wife. Families have been coming here for picnics and fishing ever since. You can walk inside the whale, right through its open mouth!

Have you ever seen a barn like *this*? The Arcadia Round Barn in Arcadia, Oklahoma, was built in 1898. The farmer who built it soaked wooden boards in water, then bent the wet boards into curves to form the walls and rafters. You can go inside to see the barn's beautiful dome.

When modern US interstate highways were built in the 1950s, they didn't go through many of the towns along Route 66. Without people driving by to shop and eat, businesses suffered. But these days, new Route 66 roadside attractions keep *popping* up—such as the 66-foot-tall pop bottle just down the road from the Arcadia Round Barn.

Pops 66 Soda Ranch fuels the spirit of Route 66 with fizzy sodas of every flavor. At night, road-trippers can see the giant bottle lit up from miles away!

Nighttime on Route 66 sure looks magical with its glowing neon signs! They show travelers where to eat, shop, and stay . . .

. . . and keep them company along the way.

Welcome to Cadillac Ranch in Amarillo, Texas! Have you ever seen anything like it? It's *sculptures*, y'all, in an outdoor museum! It's public art—and that means you're allowed to spray some paint on these big ol' Cadillac cars, if you please!

We've made it to New Mexico—known as the Land of Enchantment. The state is home to twenty-three Native American tribes, pueblos, and nations.

Acoma Pueblo stands atop a 367-foot-high sandstone mesa, sixty miles from Albuquerque. It's regarded as the oldest continuously inhabited community in the US. The Acoma people have been living here, in earthen homes, since at least the twelfth century! You can take a walking tour of the mesa, led by a Native Acoma guide.

Below, at the Sky City Cultural Center and Haak'u Museum, you can learn about Acoma's living history. And you'll see the beautiful pueblo pottery, which is known all over the world.

Historic Old Town, Albuquerque's first neighborhood, is a perfect place to take a stroll. It goes back to 1706, when a group of Spanish families settled here.

Around the shady plaza, you can admire beautiful old buildings, enjoy performances of traditional Mexican folk dancing, shop for souvenirs, and eat spicy New Mexican food, served up with red and green chiles!

I love to visit the Painted Desert, near Holbrook, Arizona. It's named for the colors—red, blue, yellow, white, and even lavender—in the rock there.

Petrified Forest National Park is located within the Painted Desert. You can walk along trails and see logs that turned from wood to stone more than 200 million years ago!

Next stop, California!

Ahhh! The Pacific Ocean breeze makes me feel cool all the way down to my hubcaps. We've reached the Santa Monica Pier in Southern California, folks—a fun place to play and the end of the Route 66 trail.

Keep on exploring, and I'll look for you 'round the bend!